A PARENT/CHILD MANUAL

IT'S O.K. TO BE GIFTED OR TALENTED!

JOEL ENGEL

Illustrated by Vaccaro Associates/Gita Lloyd

TOR

PAPERBACKS FOR EDUCATORS
426 West Front Street
Washington, Missouri 63090
(800) 227-2591 (314) 239-1999

The PARENT/CHILD MANUALS
published by Tor Books

It's O.K. to be Different
It's O.K. to Say No!
It's O.K. to Say No to Drugs!
The Parent/Child Manual on Divorce
The Parent/Child Manual on Peer Pressure
Sometimes It's O.K. to be Afraid
Sometimes It's O.K. to Tell Secrets!

All the characters and events portrayed in this book are fictitious, and any resemblance to real people or events is purely coincidental.

IT'S O.K. TO BE GIFTED OR TALENTED!

Copyright © 1987 by RGA Publishing Group, Inc.

All rights reserved, including the right to reproduce this book or portions thereof in any form.

A TOR Book
Published by Tom Doherty Associates, Inc.
49 West 24 Street
New York, NY 10010

Cover art and text illustrations by Vaccaro Associates/Gita Lloyd

ISBN: 0-812-59477-0   Can. ISBN: 0-812-59478-9

Library of Congress Catalog Card Number: 87-50881

First edition: January 1988
First trade paperback edition: March 1989

Printed in the United States of America

0 9 8 7 6 5 4 3 2 1

Introduction

The birth of a baby is a time for celebration. Parents are filled with feelings of joy and hope. Their newborn represents a future of unlimited possibilities and potential. This particular child, says each new parent, could find a cure for cancer, become President, or put an end to wars.

But in truth, all babies are not born equal. As the child grows and his personality begins to emerge, individual limitations become increasingly apparent. Not every child can be an Einstein, a Rembrandt, a Shakespeare. Only a very few are destined for greatness.

This book was written for that smaller number of children who possess the potential to achieve at levels above the norm. These are the ones who have been granted, through their gifts or talents, the ability to accomplish goals that many of us find beyond our capacity. These are the ones who may someday be written of and talked about, as they redefine the boundaries of human knowledge and experience.

But just as every seed planted in a garden does not flower, neither does every gifted and talented child achieve his or her potential. Some children's gifts languish unused.

Parents are the most important factors in helping children to use to the fullest the gifts they've been given. At times, trying to keep up with a child's seemingly inexhaustible supply of energy and curiosity, parents may find themselves wishing that the child was, well, maybe a bit more average. But a parent can derive great pride and satisfaction from helping their children to develop into wondrous human beings.

As a parent, you want the best for your child, and you want to do your best for your child. You may find yourself wondering just what your role is as the parent of a gifted or talented child, or you may be anxious about handling your gifted child properly. The purpose of this book is to alleviate your doubts and fears and arm you with the knowledge you need to make informed decisions.

Chapter One

What Is a Gifted and Talented Child?

Professionally, the terms *gifted* and *talented* apply to children whose intellectual development is greatly accelerated, or whose high achievement levels, creativity, or leadership abilities exceed the range considered to be "normal." Still other children may be gifted physically, meaning that their athletic skills far surpass those of their peers.

Diagnosing giftedness, through specific testing and professional observation, does not usually begin until the third or fourth grade. However, long before professionals get involved, most gifted and talented children exhibit a broad array of behaviors that parents can use to make their own diagnosis. Because they know their child better than anyone else, parents are the best at detecting differences between their child and others of the same age.

For parents who cannot wait until the school system gets involved to have their suspicions substantiated professionally, private psychologists are available to test even very young children. Such tests are usually expensive, however, and most parents opt not to take this route unless something appears to be wrong with the child. For the vast majority, their own observations of their child's behavior are sufficient.

The gifted child often possesses a deeper curiosity than his chronological peers. For instance, when he or she passes a mailbox, he or she may ask what it is. For most kids, the answer that the blue box is where people post their mail suffices. But the gifted child has to know who picks up the letters, the method by which the letters are sorted, who does the sorting, who delivers them, and what's in them.

The gifted child's curiosity frequently knows no bounds—but a parent's patience does. His or her persistent "whys" may drive you batty, particularly when you find that you don't know the answer in detail—even if the question is about a common occurrence. Don't ever be afraid to say that you don't know, because gifted children can sometimes see right through your made-up explanations. Make it a point, and thereby set an example, to say that the two of you will find the answer together, even if you have to go to external sources. And as you and your child visit libraries and museums, you will learn about life—and each other.

This fascination with life's mysteries can also be seen in the gifted child's passion for collecting—for choosing a subject and avidly pursuing all information and examples he or she can find. Many children, gifted or not, display an infatuation with dinosaurs—and in paleontologists we see the result of childhood "hobby" transformed into adult enthusiasm.

Often a child's neatly ordered collections will be surrounded with what looks like a major mess to parents, yet the children themselves know where everything is located. What may look like chaos to you is their order. What to you may be only a pile of junk in the corner of the room is to them a "city."

Another clue to a child's giftedness may be an unusually high energy level. The gifted child's interest in the world creates a nearly bottomless appetite for discovery. He or she may feel that sleeping, or even resting, is a waste of time that could be spent counting the number of scales on the fish in the pond behind the house, or building a skyscraper out of Mom's and Dad's shoes. He or she does not want to "miss anything" by sleeping.

Researchers believe that gifted children actually need less sleep than average-learning children. You and your weary bones may have already discovered that. Some parents mistakenly believe that their energetic child suffers from hyperactivity, when in fact the child is really gifted.

While some gifted and talented children—like many average-learning children—do not speak in well-formed sentences until they are four or five years old, many seem to move very quickly from "Da-Da" and "Ma-Ma" to valedictorian. Each day they pick up new words and phrases and incorporate them into their vocabulary. The resulting speech, coming from such precocious little mouths, can be surprising. I once saw a young woman and her two-and-a-half-year-old daughter in an elevator. The elevator was full, each passenger quiet, staring at the floor indicator above the doors, when the silence was broken by the little girl. Without hesitation, she said quite loudly, "Mother, I really must move a bowel." The poor woman's face turned red as a beet amid the laughing and snickering.

Another manifestation of giftedness can be the child's ability to pick up concepts very quickly. While adults can talk around most children with vague references, gifted children often grasp the intended meaning and may even question the adults about their circumlocution. "Why are you talking about Aunt Edythe's skin condition that way?" the child may ask.

Euphemisms also provide them with fodder for questioning authority. If you say that Aunt Edythe passed away, the child may say, "Oh, you mean she died."

By the same token, the gifted child often possesses a sense of humor you might imagine to be beyond his or her years. These children laugh at jokes other children their age miss. One young boy was categorized as "weird" by his classmates after he asked them a riddle, told them the answer, then laughed long and hard alone. "What happened to the woman who swallowed her spoon?" he asked, answering, "She could not stir." His classmates didn't understand that stirring could apply to both a spoon and a person; the boy thought it was absolutely the cleverest thing he'd ever heard.

This sort of wit and comprehension may be acquired through extensive reading. Whether or not they learn to read earlier than other children, gifted children clearly enjoy expanding their vocabulary. They are fascinated by words and their meanings. Many gifted children begin reading considerably earlier than their chronological peers, though that ability depends to a large extent upon their parents, who must devote the necessary time and expose the child to books. In any case, "See Spot run" is quickly replaced by more sophisticated works.

Because of their advanced rate of learning, gifted children often seem to their teachers to be bored in class. The reason for their behavior is simply that it takes them only one or two examples to comprehend what their classmates need twenty examples to understand. Some even fall asleep in class and wind up in trouble. After a while, they may just turn off and allow their grades to drop.

Many such children are unfortunately mislabeled by the school system as either unintelligent or troublemakers, and they go through their education without being given the chance to reach their potential. If parents step in early enough and meet with school personnel to give their observations, rather than rely on the system to handle the situation, these children receive the proper attention. It is vitally important that the parent become the child's advocate. Education without parental input can be likened to a car operating on only one cylinder.

Tony, eight, was an unusually bright boy, but was getting poor grades because he lacked interest in school. Alone in his apartment every day after school, waiting for his single-parent working mother to arrive, he taught himself to read, do math tables, and study history, all on a level far surpassing his classmates. Because of this, his mind wandered in class. Fortunately, his teacher had the common sense to call his mother into a meeting, at which Tony's mother was able to tell the teacher that she and Tony often discussed subjects that were so advanced that she was surprised he was learning them in school. In fact, Tony was learning them on his own. Thanks to the meeting, Tony was skipped ahead one grade, where, dealing with subjects closer to his achievement level, he again became interested in schoolwork.

Sometimes parents of gifted children, especially those who are not themselves gifted, are reluctant to act unless they are lucky enough, like Tony's mother, to be confronted with the matter because someone senses a problem. Parents wonder how they can possibly have produced such an amazing, even intimidating, creature. Well, the fact is that the genes that determine our individual makeups and talents bounce around like balls in a pinball machine. It is not unheard-of for a couple to have both a gifted child and a developmentally disabled one.

Parents faced with raising a retarded child will almost always take the initiative and act with authority, seeking the advice of experts and placing the child in a situation that will meet his or her needs. Similarly, the parent of a gifted child must not be overwhelmed by the task at hand. A gifted child needs as much parental support and guidance as a disabled one. If your child has exhausted your book collection at home, see to it that he or she is made aware of the public library. Then there are museums, the theater, art galleries, the natural world. Each of these will provide stimulation and entertainment. Remember that no one knows your child better than you do, and no one is better equipped to judge him or her.

When the time comes for giftedness testing, your parental input will likely be a major factor in the professional determination. Other factors will be the observation and recommendations of your child's teacher, and of course, test results. While an I.Q. test is not, by itself, the most accurate assessor of giftedness or intelligence, it does provide a standard of measurement that can be judged in conjunction with other criteria. These days, I.Q.'s of at least 130 are considered to be indicative of giftedness.

Many parents want to test their child almost as soon as he or she can walk, and, following the initial diagnosis, they may submit their child to what seems, especially to the child, to be an unending series of subsequent tests designed to pinpoint a particular area of ability. The dangers in allowing test after test are at least twofold: one, the child may begin to feel that he or she is nothing more than a laboratory guinea pig, and two, the child, numbed by a stream of tests, will consciously shut down his or her faculties, rendering the results invalid.

One thing to keep in mind at all times is that your child may have an I.Q. of 185, but he or she is still six, seven, eight years old and still a child emotionally. I bring this up because many parents, astonished and infatuated by their gifted child's brilliance or accomplishments, forget that they're the ones in charge.

Sam was six years old and read on an eleventh-grade level. Although his parents meant well, they were taken in by Sam's intellectual capabilities and let him walk all over them. Sam would argue for something he wanted to do, such as staying up late to watch television. His parents would at first say no, explaining that he must read and then go to bed. Though other kids might argue emotionally, demanding that they want this "because!", Sam could stand before his parents with a rationale as eloquent as any trial lawyer's. "It's hypocritical of you to say that I have to read when you guys watch TV all the time," he told them. Unable to counter his arguments, his parents usually gave in. Eventually, however, owing to a lack of parental supervision,

Sam became so insufferable that he needed intense psychological help.

Sam's parents had forgotten that Sam was just a little kid. Though he seemed mature, he lacked the judgment and experience to make important life decisions. That job has to be the parents', and it must apply as vigorously to gifted children as to average-learning ones. Of course, there is room for a type of democratic rule in which minor points, such as when to go to bed, can be debated. In fact, many researchers contend that this method of parenting promotes creativity in children, as opposed to the "iron fist" method, which may restrict a child's natural desire to explore and learn for himself. But the final say must belong to the parent, who should never be afraid to use the old standby "Because I told you so, and I'm the parent."

If your child is indeed gifted, you have reason to be proud. His or her energy, enthusiasm, wit, brightness, creativity, and freshness will be more of an inspiration than a chore to you. Raising a gifted child is nothing short of a challenge, but if you remember always that behind that shiny veneer of maturity and precociousness is a child like almost any other, your job will be made easier.

Chapter Two

Developing the Potential

Nancy was nine years old and had just taken, along with the rest of her class, a series of intelligence tests to determine her future academic placement. Nancy had always been an average student at best, so her counselor, Mrs. Lowe, was surprised by Nancy's results, which placed her in the top two percent of her class. Mrs. Lowe called Nancy in for a meeting and asked her what subjects she liked best. "I don't know," Nancy responded. "What are you good at?" Mrs. Lowe asked. "Nothing," Nancy said, staring at the ground.

Against her better professional judgment, Mrs. Lowe enrolled Nancy in a special program for gifted and talented students. Nancy failed miserably—not because she didn't have the ability, but because she received no encouragement at home.

Each of us has tremendous potential, and most of us develop and use only a small percentage of our abilities. What a tragedy that is, but when a gifted or talented child fails to achieve his or her fullest potential, that tragedy is even greater.

Nancy is not an isolated example. Every year, gifted minds like hers are wasted through neglect. Nancy could possibly still develop her potential, but that likelihood diminishes with each passing year.

"Use it or lose it," the researchers studying gifted and talented young people often say. Potential is like a muscle: it either grows strong from use or atrophies from lack of it. The human mind needs stretching and exercise in order to become stronger. That is as true for average minds as for gifted and talented ones. The difference between a gifted child and an average one is that the gifted child will develop more quickly and be able to go in directions the average child can't.

It does not matter what your child's genetic program is—even if it spells superintelligence—if he or she is not given any opportunities to develop it.

Your job, as a parent, is to see to it that your child's enormous potential does not go to waste. You must provide guidance in shaping his or her at-home education, which will in turn play a major role in shaping his or her attitude toward school and, in turn, accomplishment in life. By creating the sort of environment in which an inquisitive mind can find satisfaction, and an insatiable quest for information find outlets, you will be helping your child to reach his or her potential.

How do you do that? First, simply follow your child's lead. Watch to see what he or she is interested in, and try to share some of his or her enthusiasm by encouraging those interests.

Children are highly excited about the world around them. They can take great pleasure from an object as mundane as a garden hose. If your child discovers sea shells, for instance, show him or her books on the subject—if your child does not read on the book's level, read to him or her—he or she will be fascinated with the pictures—or take him or her to the aquarium if there's one nearby. And if you can get to the seashore to look for shells, by all means do that.

Expose your child to as many different ideas and places as possible. Let him or her pick and choose whatever tickles his or her fancy. Museums, art galleries, libraries—and any place geared toward a child's interests and enthusiasm—offer an almost unlimited wealth of new subjects that will stimulate a child's natural propensity for learning. A daily newspaper is a wonderful source of information for children. Concerts—all kinds of music, from rock to classical—enrich a child and may get the child interested in playing an instrument. And live theater, that most wonderful and stimulating experience, generally enthralls gifted children, who are fascinated by the actors, scenery, lighting, and the encompassing logistics; excellent theater may be found not only on a professional level but through neighborhood groups, local colleges, and high schools.

The parents' role is to guide the child to resources that may interest him or her, but without forcing a particular bias. Gifted children, even more so than average-learning children, must be allowed to develop their own preferences—and thus an identity—which are distinct from the parents'. It's all right to expose your gifted child to whatever field you find particularly fascinating or interesting, but do it gently, not emphatically. And don't worry that your child doesn't seem to pick out the most "educational" bits of information from each activity; he or she may be absorbing information on a level invisible to you.

The latest research indicates that children who are most exposed to adult-level thought and speech tend to do better intellectually than other children. That means that parents who share their own thoughts, interests, and experiences with their children have an enormous impact on the children's intellectual development.

Many parents worry that their child will not find what they have to say interesting, because they believe that the child is smarter than they are, or they become concerned that they aren't doing enough to stimulate the child. For the most part, their worries and anxieties are unfounded or easily remedied.

Tommy's mother became so concerned that he might not be getting the kind of guidance from her that she thought he needed that she contacted a counselor for help. "What kinds of things do you do with Tommy?" the counselor asked her.

"Well, we go everywhere he wants to go, pretty much," she said. "And do everything—within reason—that he wants to do."

"What's wrong with that?" the counselor asked.

"For one thing, I think Tommy's smarter than I am," she said. "I don't know how to handle that."

"He may very well be. Tommy's an unusually bright child. He has the capacity to learn quite a bit."

"So how can I teach him anything?" his mother asked. "I have nothing to offer him."

The counselor explained that just being with Tommy, talking to him about the things she did know, answering whatever questions she could, and promising to help him find out the things she didn't know were all that could possibly be expected of her—and all that Tommy would need. "You don't have to be an encyclopedia to Tommy," the counselor said. "You just have to make sure he knows what an encyclopedia is and where he can find it when he wants one."

Nadine's mother sought advice because she, too, felt that she wasn't offering her gifted child enough. "We don't seem to have much to talk about together," she said. "I keep feeling that whatever I say to her isn't smart enough."

"What do you try to talk about?" the counselor asked.

"Politics, history, things like that."

"Do you have an interest in politics and history?"

"No, not really."

"Does Nadine?"

"No, I don't think so."

"Then why are you trying to talk about them? I'm sure she senses your lack of enthusiasm for the subjects. Wouldn't it be better to share some of the things you do know about?"

"Like what?"

"Why don't you tell her about your family history? That might stimulate her interest in genealogy. Or when you go to buy clothes with her, tell her what the fashions were like when you were her age."

"What if she asks me a question I don't know the answer to?"

"Then you can find it out together," the counselor said.

Family and friends can be a wonderful resource. If your Uncle Harry is a particularly good storyteller, for example, try to arrange some time for him and your child to be together. Harry can weave all the tall tales that once captivated you and other members of your family—and you might enjoy hearing them again, too! You might also see to it that others who have interesting jobs, or have traveled extensively, share their experiences with your child.

By exposing your child to a wealth of thoughts and subjects, you are planting seeds, some of which will take root and some not. Children learn by example. They often watch adults to emulate grown-up behavior and attitudes. And gifted children are the most observant children. If they see that you, their parents, are eager to learn and try new things and are willing to say, "I don't know but I'll find out," they will follow suit.

Sometimes parents find it unnerving to see their children devouring new projects and interests, soaking up a steady stream of information with a seemingly inexhaustible supply of energy. Some parents liken their children to Frankenstein's monster: something they have created but something beyond their authority and wildly out of control. Since everything excites these children, they want to do everything—sometimes all at once.

If necessary, try instituting some "time management." Sit down with your child and have him or her decide which activities are most important to him or her. When the list is complete, allocate time for each activity according to its importance. Your child may independently discover that there are only twenty-four hours in a day, and that some of his or her interests may have to be placed on the back burner for a while, even dropped. This exercise will help him or her to focus on his or her strongest areas of interest.

A type of program that has been particularly successful for parents who live in areas where the school system does not offer special classes for the gifted and/or those whose children are too young for the school system's program, is parent-created curriculum enhancement. The parents of several gifted children can form a group that hires qualified teachers to teach specialized classes to their children after school hours. Classes that might never be offered in school—like magic, art theory, storytelling, to name just a few—can be offered to the children. If each parent had to do this on an individual tutorial basis, the cost would be prohibitive.

Such a group not only enriches the child's education, keeping him or her interested in learning in a way that regular school may not, but also allows the parent to meet regularly with other parents and compare notes on their talented children.

Gifted children very often receive more parental encouragement than other, average-learning children. If your child has an idea that seems only half-baked or ill-conceived, rather than criticize the whole concept—"Your idea isn't any good, try something else"—gently and affectionately offer some suggestions to make it better. Perhaps the idea only needs some shaping. Remember that gifted and talented children are usually very sensitive. Discouraging words can fall upon them with crushing weight. And the next time, they will be less likely to want to try something creative.

Penny, who had an interest in journalism, wanted to start a newspaper exclusively for the kids in her neighborhood. It would, she planned, give an accounting of all the news important to kids, as well as provide a listing of the nearby recreational opportunities open to them—movies, plays, puppet shows, etc. Her father, hearing the idea for the first time, instantly dismissed it as "impossible. We don't have that kind of money. Printing costs money, and we can't afford it."

Penny was heartbroken. Her father's harsh criticism had stifled her industriousness. Rather than dismiss the whole idea, he could have tried to work with her on the project, suggesting, perhaps, that she try to sell advertising to the merchants whose businesses might prosper from the endeavor, or even to parents who could invite children to birthday parties through the newsletter rather than by sending out invitations.

But even if the project was, after discussion between them, deemed impossible, at least Penny would have reached the decision herself. Her creative fervor intact, she would have been ready to attack another endeavor, this time with knowledge that could help make it a reality.

Creativity is the hallmark of gifted and talented children. As such, their creative tendencies must be exercised as faithfully as any other aspect of their education. Fortunately for parents, creative games are generally the least expensive, the most fun, and the most readily available of all. The idea is simply to have the child invent things. Tell the child to draw a vehicle that can travel through time, then have him or her explain to you why it can do that. Or give the child a paper clip with the instructions to think up, say, ten things that can be done with it. Almost any everyday item can be given to a child and used to enhance his or her creative tendencies.

Your goal, with these creative games, is to have your child explore his or her imagination, and thus stretch his or her mind. A gifted child quickly discovers that there is not just one solution to most problems; there are several.

In our society, young children are not taken very seriously. They are not given many opportunities to engage in solving problems. But gifted children seem to be more plugged into world events and news than average-learning children. They are concerned with social ills much earlier in life than other children are. Parents should listen to their gifted children as they express their opinions about, and sometimes solutions for, the problems besetting us all.

And although their methods of solving problems will probably be idealistic, simplistic, and unlikely to work, just listen. He or she may be tapped into something that the more cynical among us miss. Samantha Smith, the little girl from Maine who wrote a letter to the Soviet premier and then traveled as a world peace emissary until her death, certainly had a major impact on world events, all because she believed that her message of peace was important.

Chapter Three

Finding a Balance—Caring for the Gift

Allen was always the brightest student in his class. His mother and father, both immigrants to the United States, were eager for their son to get the most out of his education so that he would "amount to something, be a success in life." They constantly pushed Allen to do better.

At four points in his schooling, Allen's teachers recommended that he skip a grade. In their single-minded devotion to Allen's "success," his parents agreed to each acceleration.

By the time he was nineteen years old, Allen had graduated Phi Beta Kappa from a prestigious university, and within two years he had attained unquestionable success in his profession.

Now in his fifties, Allen is an unhappy and unfulfilled man. Having spent his youth in school or doing schoolwork, he never learned any social skills, nor did he cultivate any outside interests. His classmates were always years older and had nothing in common with Allen. Although he eventually married and had children, his relationships were sadly empty because he could never relate to his family as well as he could to his work.

Is Allen a success? As a professional, yes. As a human being, no. From his parents Allen learned that money and prestige could buy happiness. Years later, he learned that his parents were wrong.

Allen's story is not included here to frighten, but rather to provide a vivid illustration of the type of dilemma that many parents and their gifted children face.

Helping your child to develop his or her potential to the fullest doesn't mean that you have to encourage his or her talents in one direction at the expense of all others. No one who has only a single dimension to his or her personality can be truly happy or successful in life. Only children who develop well-rounded personalities and a strong sense of self-esteem will grow up to appreciate the richness that life offers.

The question of academic acceleration arises in many homes in which there is a gifted or talented child. Acceleration is not automatic: after the school recommends the child as a candidate, the parents make the final decision.

Certainly, there are no hard-and-fast rules on deciding to let the child skip a grade. The most important factor to consider is whether the child is being challenged by his or her education. As we have already seen, a student who is constantly bored in class is likely to turn off in an effort to numb the tedium.

If the school system does not have a specialized curriculum for gifted children, and the only alternative seems to be acceleration, you must weigh the advantages of challenging the child mentally against the disadvantages of removing him or her from his or her age group. Curriculum enhancement outside of school is a very powerful tool to augment a child's education, and allows him or her to stay in class with chronological peers.

The child's emotional maturity is another strong factor. Some children may be intellectually capable of accelerating, yet lack the emotional skills to adapt to the environment. Talk over the situation with the child's current teacher and other educators at the school, as well as the teacher in whose class he or she will be placed. Involve the child in the decision-making process. The final decision, of course, is yours, to be made after considering all the options. But remember that no decision is etched in stone. Should the accelerated child's emotional or social growth seem to be suffering too much, counseling and tutoring can be made available; at the end of the school year the advancement can be reassessed.

Some parents, in their zeal to see their children perform well in school, and measuring performance by high grades, inadvertently communicate to their children that they are loved only when they bring home good marks. In homes where the child's special ability is, say, musical, they may give the impression that only prodigies are worthy of their love. Obviously, this is the wrong impression to give to children whom we want to grow up to be happy and well adjusted.

If you overencourage any single ability—intellectual, musical, etc.—to the exclusion of other talents and interests, you are likely to communicate to your child that he or she is accepted only for his or her performance in that field. Children must know that they are loved unconditionally, for their weaknesses as well as their strengths.

Many gifted or talented children and their parents make the mistake of feeling that their particular gifts or talents should enable them to skate through life with the appropriate rewards falling into their laps. The classic example of that is the athlete with visions of million-dollar contracts dancing in his imagination. Spending all his time on the playgrounds and playing fields honing his skills, he neglects his cerebral education, feeling confident that he has what it takes to make it as a professional.

If he does succeed as a pro, terrific. But in reality his chances are infinitesimally slim. And when he discovers that he probably will never be an idolized millionaire, he faces a bleak future because he doesn't have the skills necessary to succeed in any other area. The same thing happens to those who are artistically or musically gifted and devote all their time to a single field.

In everyone's life there have to be compromises made between pursuing specific goals and developing general social, physical, emotional, and intellectual skills. Allowing a child's talents to go unfulfilled is an unfortunate waste, but to alienate him or her from society may be worse still. Children must come to know both their strengths and their weaknesses. No one is perfect, no one is strong in all areas. That lesson, too, must be part of their education.

Frequently, gifted or talented children who have always done well in particular fields are reluctant to try anything new for fear of failure. In a way, we set them up for failure by identifying them as gifted. Gifted or talented is what they conceptualize themselves as, and often they attempt only those things they already know they are good at.

Your child's self-perception is formed in large part by how others perceive him or her. A gifted or talented child who has been treated with greater deference than average-ability children because of his or her special skills is likely to feel worthwhile only when he or she performs according to expectations. Anything other than optimum performance may provoke feelings of anxiety and reluctance. Our society, in which intelligence is measured by academic standing, and athletic and artistic performances, are competitions, sends children the message that results are everything; in movies, on television, in newspapers, the message is implicit: winners are rewarded. So, afraid of not living up to past standards, many gifted or talented children do not enjoy the kinds of success and growth that would come from taking chances.

Your job as the parent of a gifted child is to convey to him or her that taking risks and chances—exploring new territory—is valuable, and that one can learn from failure as well as success, from mistakes as well as triumphs. You can do that by setting a good example, by trying new things yourself. If you fail at your new ventures and do it gracefully, your child will learn that it is the trying that's important.

Some parents say, "If my kid is going to get into Harvard, it doesn't matter if he can hit a baseball, dance, or play the oboe. What matters is that he gets good grades."

Well, as the admissions officers of major universities have begun to discover, well-rounded students tend to contribute much more to campus life, and enrich the university, than students who have perfect grade point averages. As one educator said, "Straight-A students are a dime a dozen. I'm interested in someone who has many facets in addition to good grades."

Balance is the key word. That applies to all people, but it is especially true for these special children. On the whole, they tend to be more sensitive than other children. Their highs and lows are often more exaggerated than those of average-ability children, and they react much more intensely to events. To draw an analogy: unlike a normal passenger vehicle (the average child) which will usually come to a safe stop after a flat tire, a race car (the gifted child) that suffers a blowout at 200 miles per hour will be sent hurtling out of control.

Balance. While some gifted children will take the message of success and pursue it with single-minded devotion, others react to that pressure by withdrawing. Rather than strive to be the best, they decide, consciously or not, to waste their potential. We call these children underachievers.

George had never earned less than an A in a class until the sixth grade, when he got a B in art. He probably shouldn't have gotten even that high a grade, because he was unable to draw a straight line without a ruler. Nonetheless, his father chose not to see that his son was not another Van Gogh, and blamed the teacher for George's low grade.

A short time after that, George told his father about a science project he was planning. His father, anxious to help his son in school, became too involved in the project and ended up building most of it himself without George's assistance or input. Although George got an A on the project, he felt no sense of pride; all he sensed was the pressure on him to earn high marks at any cost.

Gradually, George's grades began to slip, not so much that his teachers questioned the change, but just enough to lower his father's and his own expectations of success and reduce the pressure on him.

Some children in George's position, determined to prove to their parents that they can succeed, might have chosen the opposite route. What caused George to pull away was a combination of factors, the most powerful of which was the pervasive feeling that his father loved him only for his achievements. By smudging his record, he was punishing his father and at the same time testing his father's love.

In addition, George realized that as long as his grades remained high, there would be strong pressure on him to keep them high in all subjects, even those in which he obviously didn't excel. George's father thought his son should be outstanding in everything he tried. What he failed to realize was that George was a human being, not a perfect assemblage of unblemished parts.

In his heart, George's father felt that he was doing the right thing by encouraging his son to strive for greatness, but actually he was choking off George's self-esteem. Knowing that George had both the potential and the opportunity he did not, perhaps his father wanted George to surpass his own station in life. Or perhaps the man was trying to live out his own unfulfilled ambitions through his son. That, too, is a relatively common occurrence in homes with gifted and talented children.

As a little girl, Tina was often complimented on her beauty by complete strangers. Her mother, herself a handsome woman, eventually grew obsessed with the idea that Tina should be a beauty pageant winner. To that end, she forced Tina to take dance, piano, and elocution lessons. Tina had little or no time to spend with her friends.

No matter how well Tina did, she never felt that her mother's love was for her, for who she was, but was for the person her mother wanted her to be. Once, during a piano recital, Tina forgot how to play her chosen piece. Crying, she ran offstage into the wings, expecting her mother to join her there. But her mother waited until the recital was over, and then, instead of comforting Tina, told her how mortified she was, how Tina had embarrassed her.

Tina and her mother fought bitterly for months when Tina refused to take any more piano lessons. Eventually, Tina prevailed. Her mother, though, remained committed to Tina's entry in beauty pageants. Tina went along with the idea reluctantly.

When the big day came and Tina did not win, her mother took the loss as a personal affront, as though Tina had done it purposely to hurt her. She didn't speak to Tina for two days.

Needless to say, Tina grew up with only the barest trace of self-esteem. Unquestionably a beautiful woman, she thinks of herself as homely, and in general she lacks self-respect, confidence, and ambition.

The line between encouragement and punishment is a fine one. Parents must be careful not to obscure it further by confusing their own selfish motives with the more selfless ones of seeing their children attain their just rewards. Tina's mother failed to see that Tina was not an extension of her, but a completely separate individual.

For most parents, determining when to push and when to pull back is a more delicate matter. Some children credit their parents for pushing them, for example, to play the piano, and others claim that they probably would have played the instrument had not their parents pushed them so hard. No one can decide for you how much to push, or when; only you know your child well enough to make an informed decision. The best you can do is to make sure that your child has enough information about the good and bad consequences of his or her actions to participate in the decision-making process. That way, the child feels that he or she has some control over his or her life. Trying to inflict a "perfect" existence on your child by making all decisions for him or her, will keep your child from learning to face life realistically.

Self-esteem is the greatest single factor in a child's success. As long as your child feels loved by you—unconditionally, outside of his or her achievements or lack thereof—he or she will make your decisions easier by choosing a correct path—correct for the child, that is.

The enormous potential that has been granted to your child is a gift. You must nurture that gift and care for it so that it can be fulfilled. The kinds of opportunities and enrichment that develop well-rounded personalities will help the child to realize who he or she is and who he or she can be. Then he or she can begin to give back to the world the gift that was given to him or her.

Chapter Four

Problems Giftedness May Cause Within the Family

Each person's life impacts on and is impacted on by other lives—from those on the periphery, such as the grocer and your doctor, to those with whom you are intimately involved. Quite obviously, we make the biggest impression on those we are closest to. For most people, that means their families.

Like all families, a family in which there is a gifted and talented child can expect its share of problems. For better and for worse, gifted and talented children make indelible impressions on those who know them well.

While some gifted and talented children may feel that they are either superior or inferior to their peers, most do not generally believe themselves to be different from ordinary children; in fact, socially and emotionally they can be identical to the others. They look at themselves in the mirror and see an image that conforms, more or less, to the image of their classmates. They are happy, scared, excited, sad, angry—in short, they are all the things that other children are. It is only when they interact with others that their specialness surfaces. And therein lies the potential for problems within the family.

Julian was eight years old and unusually bright for his age. His brother, Phil, was nine and average in every way. People were always making a fuss over Julian, whereas Phil seemed forever to be in the background. This made Julian uncomfortable because Julian loved his brother very much, and while Phil probably loved Julian equally, his resentment and jealousy over Julian's gifts and the attention they attracted caused him to pick on Julian as a defense mechanism. Phil bossed Julian around and ridiculed him at every turn. Julian was hurt by Phil's maliciousness, but he endured it because he felt guilty over his own good fortune.

Somewhere along the line he decided that he would have to suffer for his gifts in order to balance the books.

When the boys' school recommended that Julian skip a year because he was no longer being challenged by the curriculum in his grade, his parents immediately said yes, even though that would place both brothers in the same class. His parents did consider the possibility that Phil might be subject to ridicule for having his younger brother in the same grade—especially since Julian's marks would likely be higher than Phil's—but they felt that the most important thing was Julian's education.

It was Julian who said no. He refused to place his brother in the uncomfortable situation that his acceleration would have created. Julian so much wanted his brother's love and companionship, which Phil unconsciously withheld as punishment, that he sometimes wished he were an ordinary child.

Soon thereafter, Julian's grades began to drop. Eventually, his performance had slacked off so much and so consistently that he was judged to be just another child of average ability; even if he had wanted to, Julian could not have reversed the momentum.

And his relationship with his brother? Watching Julian let his potential waste away both pleased Phil and made him contemptuous of his younger brother; Phil never gave Julian the affection and acceptance he sought.

This story highlights several problems common to families with a gifted child. The exact scenario will probably not be enacted in your household, but one or more of its components may be. So the solutions are very important.

It is the job of the parent to make sure that each child in the family is treated with equal love, care, and respect, no matter how many or few gifts he or she possesses. Every human being is special in some way and should not be compared with anyone else. While the gifted child will move faster than other children and exhibit greater potential, the parents must focus on each child's individual abilities—digging to find them, if they have to—and make him or her feel special, too.

We all come equipped with some unique gifts, which, if given an opportunity to develop, separate us from the rest. If all children were challenged to the limit of their abilities, none would feel less important than any other. And the chances of avoiding the type of jealous situation that occurred between Julian and Phil would be greatly increased.

Unfortunately, these brothers' parents made one brother more special than the other, and both paid the price. Julian's withdrawal indicated a lack of self-esteem, as well as too much pressure to do well; too few expectations and not enough pressure were placed on Phil, causing him to feel worthless and unwanted.

When the acceleration of a younger sibling could affect the delicate family balance, the entire family should be involved in the decision-making process. Knowing instinctively that acceleration was the proper move for Julian, his parents made a wise decision, but they did it without asking the brothers for their opinions or explaining the situation to them. This only accentuated the tensions between the boys and resulted in an intolerable outcome. Parents should trust their children to make wise choices once they have all the facts at hand. It is likely that if their parents had treated them with equal respect, and consulted them, Julian and Phil would have been more closely aligned and agreed to the acceleration.

In any event, leveling out the child who has the greater ability, so that he does not make the other uncomfortable, is the wrong approach. Julian's well-intended refusal turned out to do nothing for either Phil or the brother's relationship, and it was certainly a tragic waste of Julian's potential. Intelligence is a dynamic process, not something that you can hold on to and maintain at will. No child can be expected to know or understand that—but his or her parents can. The parents' responsibility is to assume the leadership role.

Some parents, in their zeal to produce gifted children, decide that any and all of their offspring should be enrolled in gifted programs. One educator likes to tell the story of a particular couple who had a "nice home, nice cars, money in the bank. 'So now we're going to have a gifted child,'" he quoted the wife as saying. When the time came, they forced the school district to place their only child, who was only slightly above average in ability, into a gifted program, where he tried frantically to keep up with other students who easily grasped the material. Despite poor grades and his protests, the couple maintained that the gifted program was where their son belonged.

As time went on, the boy grew to detest school, which was an unbearable chore, and in the process lost every bit of his self-esteem. Being constantly pitted against others who dwarfed his abilities caused him to see himself as a failure. Eventually, he dropped out.

Well-meaning parents often decide—mistakenly—that if one of their children is gifted and talented, and enrolled in a special program, that all of their children should be similarly enrolled. Again, each child should be challenged to the limits of his or her abilities—no more or less. That may mean that each child develops wildly disparate interests, requiring you to devote even more time to accompanying them to their individual lessons or clubs. But that time, parent alone with child, can help to make each child feel important in his or her own right.

Another example: Betty, nine, showed great promise on the violin. She had already mastered several pieces usually thought to be for much older, more advanced students. Her teacher told Betty's parents that she possessed the talent to be a truly superior musician who could one day fill concert halls with patrons anxious to hear her play.

Betty's father had once held similar aspirations for himself. Although he showed greater than average talent, he didn't have quite what it took to earn a scholarship to a good music school, and his family didn't have the money to pay his way through. All of his life Betty's father has felt incomplete, his unfulfilled ambition nagging him constantly.

Listening to Betty play the violin aroused conflicting emotions in him. On the one hand, he was proud of his daughter. On the other, he found himself jealous of her—jealous that she had the opportunity and talent he lacked. When she made a mistake, he screamed unmercifully at her, and when she played well, he said nothing, as if it were to be expected.

When Betty told her father that she had no plans to become a professional musician, he went into a rage, demanding that she make the most of what she had been given. Betty maintained that, although she had the talent, she didn't have the interest necessary to sustain the discipline.

Betty's father was exasperated. He had had the desire but not the talent or the opportunity, and now his daughter had the talent and the opportunity but not the desire. He continued to challenge her, to berate her; they had long, bitter arguments. Their relationship deteriorated.

Parents who find themselves overly involved in their children's pursuits must question their own motives. Some will say that they are doing it for the child's own good, but is that really true? And even if they do win out eventually, with the child pursuing the goal that the parent insisted on, the victory may be a hollow one; children who act only to please or subdue their parents may develop deep-seated resentment, which surfaces with a fury later in life.

Remember, you are not your child, and your child is not you. Each child, like each adult, has something unique to offer. Remember that your gifted child often feels different and odd. While you have the benefit of maturity to judge just how lucky your child is to be so blessed, your child may at times think of him- or herself as cursed. He or she is more sensitive than other children. He or she is constantly being singled out for his or her accomplishments, even when he or she wants to be like average kids and disappear into the background. Gifted or talented, your child is still a child, with childlike innocence and need for approval and affection. It may be confusing for you to understand this combination of child and adult, but think how confusing it is for him or her.

As the parent of a gifted or talented child, you must take each day with a great deal of humor. You have been blessed with a being whose energy, insight, and behavior challenge you constantly. Enjoy the challenge. Be careful not to succumb to the temptation to question yourself at every turn, wondering whether you're doing enough to help your child reach his or her potential. Face the task of raising this special person with the knowledge that you will do the best you can do, using all the resources you can muster. Love your child. The rest will take care of itself.

Chapter Five

Kids' Stories

On the following pages, you will find a series of stories you can read with your child that will help him or her to develop an awareness of how being gifted and talented separates him or her from other children, as well as how other children may see him or her. They will also help you to understand better how your child feels because of his or her gift, and how you, as a parent, affect him or her.

I suggest that you set aside a certain amount of time to read, going only so far as interest—yours and your child's—allows. If you like, change the names or the circumstances in the stories.

Remember, though, these stories are fiction. The characters always do the "right" thing. You will not always be as wise or as lucky.

Nevertheless, the stories are valuable. Their intent is to broaden your knowledge, enabling you and your child to make better-informed decisions.

DENISE'S STORY

Denise was nine. Her family moved from one side of town to another, so she had to change schools. In her previous school Denise had been in a special program for very bright children, but in her new school there was no such program. Denise's parents were aware of this when they moved, so they decided to further her education with specialized classes after school. Denise was excited because she would be learning about new and different things.

But Denise had some problems in school. Her classmates weren't as smart as she was.

Denise wanted to be liked so that she could make new friends. But she was afraid that when it was her turn to answer questions in class, the other kids would think she was showing off if she always got the answer right. So Denise began to miss some questions.

First, she pretended not to get her math tables right. Then she made a mistake in geography class. Denise also began to miss questions on tests so that she would not get perfect grades.

Denise's teacher knew that Denise had gotten good grades before. She assumed that Denise was having trouble now because of the trauma of moving.

Denise did make new friends very quickly and all seemed to be going well until report cards came out. Denise's parents were shocked by her lower than normal grades, so they talked to her about the situation. She admitted that she had tried to do less than her best so that she could make friends.

Her parents finally convinced her that no one would ever think badly of a person for doing her best, and Denise agreed to do her best. And you know what? When Denise started to do better all of a sudden, her friends, and everyone else in her class, were very impressed. And they all tried to keep up with her.

Have you ever tried purposely to do less than your best? Why?

MIKE'S STORY

Mike was nine when his father was transferred from a job in Arizona to another in New York City. The family really didn't want to go, but they had to. Mike said good-bye to all his friends.

In Arizona, Mike had been enrolled in a special program for the gifted and talented because he had been in the top three percent of his age group. But in New York, it turned out that Mike did not qualify for his new school system's gifted and talented program. In fact, Mike was just another bright student in his class, not even the best.

Mike had a hard time dealing with this. In Arizona he had always been near the top. Sure, there were a lot fewer kids, so the competition wasn't as strong, but nevertheless he had been special. Now, not only did he have to make friends all over again but he wasn't special anymore.

One day Mike's mother got a call from the security office of a local department store. Mike had been caught shoplifting. His mother came to pick him up.

She was very angry. "Why did you do this?" she asked. "You never did anything like this before."

Mike couldn't answer her.

In school his grades had dropped. His parents knew that something was bothering him deeply. They figured it was taking him time to adjust to his new surroundings. But Mike's grades did not improve, and he was picked up again for shoplifting three months later.

His parents were terribly unhappy.

They didn't know what to do with him. Someone at Mike's school suggested that they see a counselor.

At the counselor's office, Mike was reluctant to talk. Finally he opened up, and told the counselor that since he'd moved to New York, he felt like a nobody.

"Because there are so many people here?" the counselor asked.

"No," Mike said. "That's not it." He paused, then described what had been bothering him. "Back home I was king of the school. Everybody looked up to me. I was the smartest one there. Here, I'm nobody. I don't even qualify for the special class."

"You mean, you felt special when you were in the special class," the counselor said. Mike nodded yes. "And now that you're not in the special class, you're not special anymore."

After the counselor explained the situation to Mike's parents, they made sure that he knew that he would always be special to them, no matter which class he was in or how well he did.

Do you feel that you have to act a certain way for your parents to love you? Do you have to act a certain way for you to love yourself?

BECKY'S STORY

Becky, nine, liked to watch the news with her parents. She also read the newspaper and listened to news stations on the radio.

All the adult problems that she heard and saw and read about seemed silly to Becky. She couldn't understand how adults had made such a big mess of the world. Every time she heard about war, or hunger, or violence, she thought to herself that none of it was necessary.

After thinking long and hard about the situation, she imagined, all by herself, solutions to the world's problems. She had a solution for every bad thing that was in the news.

Every time she tried to tell her parents about her plans to make the world better, they either didn't listen or treated her as if she was just a little kid who didn't understand all the complications involved.

Eventually, Becky stopped caring about the news. When her parents watched the news on television or listened on the radio, Becky left the room. She didn't read the newspaper anymore, either.

When it finally dawned on her parents that Becky was no longer interested in the news, they asked her why. "You were always so attentive to it before," her father said.

"You didn't listen to me when I wanted to talk about it," she said.

"What didn't we want to listen to, honey?" her mother asked.

"My opinions," Becky said.

Becky's parents told her that they didn't realize they had been cutting her off. They asked her what she thought some possible solutions could be. And you know what? When she told them, they both agreed that she had some pretty good ideas.

Becky told them that when she grew up she wanted to be President of the United States so that she could fix the world's problems.

If you were President of the United States, what's the first thing you'd do?

IRA'S STORY

Ira, nine, was one of the best students in his class. He was proud of his abilities and liked to please his parents by bringing home good grades.

His problem was his grandmother. Whenever his parents went out of town, he had to stay with her. Even when they were gone for the evening, he stayed at his grandmother's apartment, which was just a few blocks from his house.

Although he loved his grandmother, he hated to stay with her. She would invite her friends to come over so that she could show off her smart grandson. With all of them standing around, he was expected to read aloud from grown-up books and recite the math tables.

Ira felt like a trained seal at a zoo. But because it gave his grandmother so much pleasure, he did what she asked for as long as he could.

One night, though, he finally had enough. In front of his grandmother and her friends, he screamed that he wasn't a puppet. Then he stormed off to his room. His grandmother was terribly upset and embarrassed.

When his parents came to pick him up, his grandmother told them that Ira had acted badly. "I don't know what got into him," she said.

Ira's parents took him home and asked for his version of the story. After Ira explained, his parents understood what had happened and didn't punish him. They told him that he should have informed them long ago about what his grandmother had been forcing him to do. Then they could have done something about it.

His mother asked him how he liked it when she yelled at him in front of his friends about something he did wrong.

"I hate it," he said.

"I'm sure your grandmother feels the same way," his mother said.

Ira agreed.

"Did you ever tell her that you didn't like it when she made you do that?" his mother asked him.

"Well, no," Ira said.

"Then how could she have been expected to know?" his father asked.

"I guess she can't read my mind," Ira said.

The next day Ira went to his grandmother's apartment and apologized to her. He explained that it made him feel funny when she asked him to show off. Then it was her turn to apologize. She told him that she hadn't known how bad it made him feel, and she promised never to ask him to do it again.

Ira learned that honesty is always the best policy.

Does someone in your family sometimes do something that makes you feel embarrassed?

MAGGIE'S STORY

Maggie, nine, was probably the best athlete in her class. She could run faster, jump higher, and throw a ball farther than anyone else.

Unfortunately, her athletic skills caused her a lot of problems. Many of the girls in her class accused Maggie either of showing off or of using her talent to get close to the boys, while most of the boys refused to play with her because she often beat them at whatever game they chose. Sometimes when they played football, a bunch of boys would gang up on her and tackle her, even though it was supposed to be touch football.

Maggie didn't care too much. She wanted to be a famous athlete when she got older. Whether she competed in track and field at the Olympics, or played professional basketball, baseball, or football, she knew that she could and would succeed. But sometimes she felt lonely.

Maggie's parents knew that their daughter was special and that her specialness was creating problems for her. They watched as she became quieter and more withdrawn. She would come home alone from school and go immediately into the backyard, where she would shoot baskets for hours.

One day Maggie's father came home very excited. He had heard from a co-worker about a club Maggie might be interested in: a sports club for boys and girls. They play all sorts of sports, he said, from soccer to baseball.

Maggie wasn't certain she wanted to join. She said she was afraid that those kids would treat her the way the kids at school did, but she agreed to at least go down to the field where they played. She would just watch them, she said, and if she liked it—well, then she'd see about joining.

As soon as she got there, Maggie knew she wanted to join. Out on the field, boys and girls of all ages were playing together. Some played baseball, some basketball, some soccer; some raced each other around the track. They all looked like good athletes. And no one cared whether you were male or female. Everyone was judged on his or her performance—nothing more.

Within a few weeks, Maggie had made some very good friends in the club. After school, she would go straight to the playing field. She didn't have to deal with the taunts and teasing of her schoolmates.

But another thing happened. Because she was so much happier now, she projected herself that way. And suddenly, her schoolmates wanted to be around her. They even asked her to play with them. So Maggie compromised. On some days she went to her club. On other days she stayed and played with the kids at school. Everyone wanted her on their team.

Have you ever felt different, or has someone ever made you feel different, because of something you could do better than anyone else?

GARY'S STORY

Gary, eight, was a very good artist. He could sculpt in clay, or paint or draw anything he saw. His parents were very proud of Gary, and they had several of his paintings, drawings, and sculptures displayed around the house.

His sister, Greta, didn't have any particular artistic talent and was extremely jealous of Gary. Every once in a while she would steal and destroy some of Gary's works of art.

Her parents always punished Greta for this behavior, telling her that she shouldn't be jealous of Gary. The more they did that, though, the more she hated Gary.

Gary didn't feel particularly gifted or

special just because he was a good artist. He hated to see Greta get in trouble. Gary tried to be nice to her, but she was always mean to him. The nicer he was to her, the meaner she got. She kept calling him names and destroying his work. Nothing he did seemed to help the situation.

Finally, Gary told his parents that he couldn't stand it anymore. He said he didn't want to create any more works of art because it hurt Greta too much.

Gary and Greta's parents decided to talk to a friend of theirs who was a guidance counselor. The counselor told them that the reason Greta was jealous was that she felt her parents loved Gary more than her.

"We love both our children just the same. We don't love Gary more just because he's a good artist," their mother said.

"Well, that's the way it looks to Greta," said the counselor.

The children's parents realized that, because Gary's talent was so obvious, they had encouraged him right from the beginning. But they had never done anything to find out what abilities Greta might have.

As it turned out, Greta had a strong interest in dance, and her parents agreed to give her lessons. Her parents soon had not only Gary's works decorating the house but photographs they'd taken of Greta performing at recitals.

If you could decorate your house with something that reflects your personality, what would it be?

LOUISE'S STORY

Louise was seven. Her parents and teacher told her that she was going to be put in a class for gifted children because the class she was in didn't meet her educational needs. Her new classmates would all be smart, and the teacher would teach material that wouldn't bore them.

But Louise liked her old class, even though she was bored, because all her friends were in it.

Louise told her parents that she refused to change classes. Her parents tried to explain that the change was for the best, that it would help her to reach her potential.

"I don't care about my potential. I just care about my friends," Louise cried.

"You don't care now because you're too young to make that kind of decision," her mother said. "But someday you will care."

"Not me," Louise insisted.

Louise was placed in the gifted class. At first her grades slipped, and she was quiet and resentful around the house. Her parents were worried that maybe the class was too hard for her, that maybe she belonged back in her old class. They voiced their concerns to the teacher. But the teacher told them to wait awhile until Louise got used to the new class.

One day after school Louise walked home with one of the girls in her class. They liked each other a lot and soon were good friends.

Louise's grades began to rise. One day she apologized to her mother about putting up such a fight about changing classes. "You know, I'm really happy now," Louise said. "I'm learning all sorts of interesting things, and I'm making good new friends. When I see my old friends, it's nice, but it's not the same as before."

Louise's mother nodded.

"How did you know it would turn out like this?" Louise asked her.

"Because, honey," her mother said, "I'm a lot older than you are and I've been through things like this a hundred times before. That's one of the good things about being an adult."

"Sometimes parents really do know best," Louise said.

Can you remember a time when your parents knew better than you did about something? What was it?

ANTHONY'S STORY

Anthony, nine, was an amateur ham radio operator. With a little help from his father, he had constructed a small but sophisticated system that enabled him to speak with other ham radio operators all over the world.

What Anthony liked most about being a ham was that his age didn't matter to anyone with whom he spoke. Old men, middle-aged women, and young boys and girls all conversed together, as equals. Anthony was learning a great deal about different people from many parts of the world. He also sometimes found out about events like an earthquake in South America and a train wreck in Europe before they made the newspapers and television the next day.

Anthony kept his equipment in his room. Sometimes late at night, when he was supposed to be sleeping, he would quietly turn on the radio. He knew that his parents would be mad if they found out he was staying up late to be on the air.

One night Anthony's father went into the kitchen for a glass of milk to help him sleep. He heard Anthony talking and immediately knew what his son was doing. Angrily, Anthony's father went into his room and told Anthony to shut off the radio. "And the next time I catch you using it after your bedtime, I'm going to take it away from you for good," he said.

"I'm sorry, Dad," Anthony said. He signed off, then turned off the radio.

"Now get to sleep," his father said.

Anthony lay in bed and thought. For the last several nights, he had been talking with a boy about his own age who lived in a small town in Canada. He and Joseph had told each other things they had never told anyone else.

Joseph's father had died when he was small, and he had no brothers or sisters. His mother worked nights, so Joseph was usually alone from the time his mother left to go to work to when she came home, early in the mornings. Joseph's radio had belonged to his father, and Joseph's mother did not like to see Joseph use the radio because it reminded her of her husband. Because of this problem and the time difference between where Anthony lived and where Joseph lived, the boys could only talk to each other after Anthony's bedtime.

Anthony did not want to lose touch with this new and special friend. The next night he set his alarm and got up around midnight. He tiptoed down the hall to make sure that his parents were asleep, then went back to his room, turned on his ham radio, and contacted Joseph. The two of them talked for a couple of hours.

This went on for a few nights, even though Anthony was tired during the days because he didn't get enough sleep. His parents didn't suspect a thing.

One night Anthony was telling Joseph about a baseball game he'd played in when he heard a terrible crashing sound and Joseph started screaming. Anthony knew there was something terribly wrong. He immediately turned to the emergency wavelength, found someone who would help, and gave them Joseph's name, address, and call number. Then he shut down the radio and went to bed, very worried about his friend.

The next day Anthony's mom said to him at breakfast, "Anthony, is something wrong? You seem a little upset this morning."

"I'm O.K., Mom," Anthony said. But he wasn't, and he was sure Joseph wasn't, either.

That evening the phone rang, and Anthony's dad answered it. The call was for Anthony. Anthony was surprised to hear Joseph's voice.

"Thanks," Joseph said. "The bookshelves fell apart, all over me and my desk and the radio. But the people you talked to came and got me out."

"Wow!" Anthony said. "Are you O.K.?"

"Busted both legs," Joseph said, "and smashed the radio." Joseph laughed. "What a mess! I'm in the hospital, but Mom says she'll buy me a new radio when I get out, and she said I could call you to let you know I was O.K."

When Anthony got off the phone, he told his parents what had happened.

"I'm very glad that Joseph is going to be all right," Anthony's father said, "and I'm proud of you for thinking so quickly of how to help him. But you did break the rules."

Anthony's father took the ham radio away for a month. But he encouraged Anthony to write to Joseph, and he and Joseph's mother worked out a schedule for the boys to radio each other.

Was Anthony right when he disobeyed his father? Was Anthony's father right to punish him?

PATTY'S STORY

Patty, seven, always did very well, both in school and in other activities. Her friends looked up to her as a leader, and her teachers told her parents that she had great potential.

Patty's parents were proud of her. They told her how much they expected of her, which was really a lot. Every time Patty did something, she felt a lot of pressure to do a perfect job.

After a while, Patty felt that she couldn't take the pressure anymore. She was tired of always having to prove herself. Anything that she did had to be as good as before, or she felt like a failure.

One day Patty made the decision not to try hard anymore. The first time she didn't do well on a test, she felt guilty. And when she brought her test paper home for her parents to see, they were disappointed. But then it got easier. Each test she did a little bit worse. She also stopped being a leader for her friends, telling them "Go find someone else."

Patty didn't like not doing as well as she could, but this feeling wasn't as bad as the feeling she had had when all the pressure was on. She thought that if she could lower everyone's expectations of her, then she would do better again, because then the pressure wouldn't be as strong.

Eventually, Patty's grades fell to just about average. Her teacher asked her if something was wrong at home. Patty said that everything was fine. She felt that she had a secret.

Then her parents sat down to talk with her. They had waited this long, they told her, because they wanted to see if she would correct the situation on her own.

"You're not doing as well as you could," her mother said.

"Can you tell us why?" her father asked.

"I just don't care anymore," Patty said. She was lying. She did care very much, but she didn't want to care.

"I know that we've put a lot of pressure on you," her father said.

"We expect so much from you. Maybe that's wrong," her mother said.

"Everybody wants me to be perfect," Patty said. "Well, I'm not perfect, I'm just me."

"But you're not like everybody else," her mother said. "You're special."

"I understand what she's saying," her father said. "She feels like she has to win at everything she does. That's a lot of pressure."

"It sure is," Patty said.

They all made a deal. Patty would try hard again, but every time she began to feel too much pressure to do well, all three of them would sit down to talk about it.

What kinds of pressure do you feel? Does it come from you or from your parents?

CHUCK'S STORY

Chuck, eight, was a computer wizard. Each day he hurried home from school so that he could sit in front of his computer. He had no friends at school because he thought they were all too dumb, and they didn't share his interest in computers.

Chuck's parents were concerned about him. Although they were glad that he had such a strong interest in computers, they would rather have seen him devote some time to other interests, and to other kids. They were afraid that he would never learn how to deal with other people.

For a few months they ignored the situation, thinking that it was just a phase Chuck was going through. But Chuck's interests never changed. His parents introduced him to other boys in the neighborhood and encouraged him to play ball with them. Occasionally, Chuck went along with this, to make his parents happy. But he did not enjoy himself, and he didn't really get along with the other kids.

When Chuck's parents threatened to take away his computer, Chuck threw a tantrum. He refused to speak to them unless they promised to let him keep the computer. Then Chuck's mom came up with an idea.

She had heard about a club for kids like Chuck who were interested in computers. If Chuck would agree to at least check out the club, they would let him have his computer back. Of course, Chuck said yes.

As soon as he walked into the room, Chuck liked it. The club was filled with other boys and girls just like him, as intensely interested in computers as he was. Without giving up his beloved computer, Chuck made new friends. And soon he and his new friends were exploring many things together, not just computers.

If you could start any sort of club, what would it be?

TERESA'S STORY

Teresa, eight, had taken some tests that identified her as gifted, and the school had placed her in a special class. When that happened, Teresa walked around to all her old friends and classmates and told them that she was smarter than they were.

Her behavior didn't make her very popular.

Even at home, Teresa started telling her brothers and sisters, and then her mom and dad, that she was the smartest of them all. No one wanted to be around her.

This went on for a few weeks. By that time, Teresa had no friends left and her family avoided her. Everything people said, she argued with, telling them that she knew better.

Then she took her first test in her new class. Teresa had told everyone that she was the smartest of the smartest, but when the results came back, Teresa only got a C. She was heartbroken and very embarrassed.

When she got home, she was very quiet. Her mom knew that something was wrong. Teresa showed her the test paper. Her mom didn't rub it in. On the one hand, she was disappointed that Teresa hadn't done better, but on the other hand, she was glad that Teresa had learned a lesson.

"What lesson?" Teresa asked.

"The lesson," said her mom, "is that there will always be someone smarter than you and someone not as smart. Life is filled with different kinds of people. No one should get too big for her britches."

Have you ever bragged about something and then been embarrassed by it? What was it?

QUENTIN'S STORY

Quentin, eight, did particularly well in school one semester, better than he ever had before. When he brought home his report card, his parents gave him presents and threw a party for him and invited all his friends. He heard them bragging to their friends about how well he had done.

Quentin liked all the attention. They had never before made such a big deal about him, so he decided to try hard all the time.

The next semester he brought home good grades again. And again his parents treated him as special.

From then on, Quentin told himself that he would always do well. He decided that his parents loved him much more when he did well.

One day Quentin got a bad grade on a test. The teacher had asked the students to take their tests home and have their parents sign them. When Quentin heard that, he started to cry and ran out of the classroom. He ran far away.

Quentin didn't come home for dinner that night. His parents were extremely upset and called some of his friends' parents and then called the police. They gave the police a description of Quentin.

A few hours later the police brought Quentin home. He had been hiding behind the grocery store. He was crying.

His parents asked him why he hadn't come home, and he told them that he was afraid they wouldn't love him anymore because he'd gotten a bad grade on his test.

"Don't you know that we will always love you?" his mom asked. "You're the most important thing in the world to us."

Quentin explained that he only felt that way when he did well. That made his parents feel like crying. They realized that they had made it seem that way to him, making such a big fuss when he did well and being quiet when he didn't.

"From now on, we want you to know that we love you no matter what," his father said. "Just do the best you can do and that's good enough for us. Don't ever be afraid to come to us. We're proud of you always."

Is it O.K. with you not to be the best at everything?

FRAN'S STORY

Fran was eight. Her piano teacher told her and her parents that she could one day be a world-famous pianist. She was already playing pieces that older students were struggling with.

The problem was that Fran didn't want to practice as much as would be necessary to reach her full potential as a musician. Instead of coming home after school every day and sitting down at the piano for three or four hours, Fran wanted to play with her friends.

Fran's mother, who had wanted to be a pianist but found that she didn't have the talent for it, kept encouraging Fran to practice. She said that she didn't care if Fran had any friends because music was more important.

Fran and her mother fought all the time, but her mother usually won out. Fran was miserable.

One day, during a lesson, Fran just wasn't concentrating. Her teacher asked her if something was wrong. Fran told her that she really wanted to be off with her friends. Then she explained about all the fights she was having with her mother.

The next day, while Fran was at school, the piano teacher dropped by to visit Fran's mother. The teacher told her that Fran had been complaining about having to practice all the time.

"But I want her to be what I couldn't be," her mother said.

The teacher told her that, as a mother, she could only be responsible for showing Fran the way and giving her the opportunity. The rest was up to Fran. "I've been teaching piano a long time, and I've never met a student who turned out to be great unless he really wanted to be," the teacher said.

That night Fran's mom and Fran had a talk. Her mom decided that she had been acting selfishly, wanting Fran to be a pianist just because it was something she had once wanted for herself. Fran's mom gave her the opportunity to practice as much or as little as she wanted to. "If you decide that a professional career is something you want, then go for it," her mom said. "The choice is yours."

Given the chance to do other things in addition to playing piano, Fran developed many interests. She became an excellent pianist, but did not play professionally.

What would you have done if you were Fran's mother?

KENNY'S STORY

Kenny, eight, was liked very much by his teacher. He was an excellent student and very well behaved. Whenever the teacher had to go out of the room for a few minutes, she put Kenny in charge. The other kids called him the teacher's pet. He thought they were just jealous.

One time when the teacher was out of the room, one of the other kids started acting up and drew some dirty pictures on the chalkboard. Kenny was trying to erase them when the teacher walked back in. She asked Kenny who had drawn the pictures.

Kenny hesitated a moment, then told her. The other boy got in trouble. Kenny felt terrible.

He felt worse when he discovered that none of the other boys would talk to him. They called him "Ratfink" and other names. He had lost all of his friends.

Kenny's father saw that Kenny was upset, and asked him why. Kenny told him what had happened.

"What I am going to tell you may not make you feel any better right now, but it is something you have to know," his father said.

"What's that?" Kenny asked.

"In life," his father said, "there are leaders and there are followers. The leaders lead and the followers follow. It's easy to be a follower, but not so easy to be a leader. Are you with me so far?"

Kenny nodded.

His father continued, "When you're a leader, you are forced to make some decisions that are not popular. Then you have a choice. If you make unpopular decisions, you have to live with the consequences. Every time you make one you risk losing friends. You have to judge for yourself if making those decisions is worth it. No law says that you had to give the teacher the name of that student. You could have kept silent. But you did what you thought was best. Next time you're in that situation, you'll have to decide all over again what to do. No one can decide for you. Only you. But remember, being a leader is a big responsibility. People may get hurt and in trouble because of something you say or do."

Kenny understood what his father was talking about. And although he was still sad about making his friends angry at him, he felt that he was special. He was a leader. The next time, he thought, he would make the right decision—even though he didn't know exactly what it would be.

The next day in school, most of the boys ignored Kenny, as they did the day after that and the day after that. Kenny still felt hurt about losing his friends, but he had learned a valuable lesson. Eventually, a few of the boys began to speak to Kenny again, and then a few more did the same. And one day Kenny was back together with his friends.

What was the hardest decision you've ever had to make?

MARIA'S STORY

Maria, ten, had been planning her entry in the school's annual science fair for nearly a year. She wanted to win the competition, but she also wanted to do something no other student would even think of.

She had gotten the idea for her project from a show she had seen on television, a program about the great advances being made in robotics. Maria thought she could create a robot at home, one that would walk and talk.

Every day when she got home from school, Maria shut herself in her bedroom to work on her project. She came out only to run down to the basement to do some soldering or to get a piece of scrap wiring.

"What are you being so mysterious about?" Maria's mother asked one day.

"I can't tell you, but it's the greatest thing I've ever tried and I know it will work," Maria said.

Maria worked hard every afternoon. Her design was all worked out and the robot was nearly complete. She still had to figure out how to get a synthetic voice box. A few weeks earlier she had seen, in a toy store, a demonstration of a very expensive new toy that had just the voice box she wanted. But Maria didn't have any money left. All of her allowance had been spent on supplies for the robot.

"Mom, I need a favor," Maria said one afternoon.

"What can I do for you?" her mom said.

"Well, I've run out of money and I just have to have something to finish my project. It's really important, Mom, and I wouldn't ask if I could figure out any other way to do it."

"How much money do you need, Maria?" asked her mother.

"A lot," she said. "What I have to buy costs sixty-five dollars. But I'll pay you back as soon as I can. Please, Mom?"

"Sixty-five dollars is a lot of money, Maria, and we don't have it to spare right now. I'm sorry. I know how important this project is to you."

"But, Mom, this is all I have left to buy, and my project is just a bunch of junk without it," Maria said. Her mom hadn't even asked what the money was for; she'd just said no.

Crying, Maria ran up to her room. She had to have that voice box! Finally, in desperation, she decided to steal it. "People steal things all the time," she thought. "I'm not stealing for fun; this is a very important project."

Maria spent the rest of the night trying to figure out how to get the toy out of the store without being caught, and a few days later she carried out her plan.

Finally, the day of the science fair arrived. Maria placed her exhibit alongside all the other kids' projects, which ranged from a depiction of how a tornado forms to a chart showing the process of plant growth. Maria kept a cloth cover on her robot until the chief judge, Mr. Stempf, reached her table.

With a flourish, Maria whipped the cover away and revealed her robot. She pushed a button on the control box and the robot walked forward, clapped its hands, and said, "Hello, how are you today?"

"Well, Maria," said Mr. Stempf, after all the exhibits had been shown, "it looks like you're the winner, hands down. You've done an incredible job and we judges are very impressed. Congratulations!"

Maria thought she'd be more excited about winning, but she felt very guilty and a little sick. She couldn't believe she had stolen a toy just to make sure her robot was perfect.

When she met her family at the car, her mother said, "I think we have some talking to do when we get home." Maria just nodded and sat quietly in the back seat.

Back home, Maria and her mother sat together in the kitchen. Maria's mom said, "Maria, I know that you built that robot with scrap from the basement, but where did you get that voice box? Was that what you needed the extra money for?"

"Oh, Mom, I stole it. I stole a toy from a store downtown and took the voice box from it for my robot."

"Maria! I can't believe you did that! What were you thinking?"

"I don't think I was thinking, Mom. I just had to have that toy for the voice box. I just went ahead and stole it. I feel pretty rotten now."

"Well, you should feel rotten. That was a rotten thing to do. This is an example of the means not justifying the end. Do you know what that means?"

"Sort of," Maria said.

"It means that if you do things you

can't be proud of, just to reach a goal, you won't be happy with yourself once you've attained that goal. Your project would have won even without the voice box. You're a bright girl and you should have known that."

"I wasn't just making the robot to win at the science fair," Maria said. "I made it to show off."

"You committed a crime, just so you could show off. Tomorrow we'll go to the store and tell them what you did and I'll pay for the toy. You'll have to work for me to pay me back."

"O.K., Mom," Maria said. She knew that her mother was right. Doing anything she could not be proud of was wrong.

Do you think what Maria did was wrong? Have you ever done something like that? Would you?

SAM'S STORY

Sam, ten, had always concentrated on school subjects. He wasn't too interested in sports until he met another boy who was one of the best athletes in the school. Their friendship introduced Sam to sports.

Sam's parents thought that sports were a waste of time. They didn't watch any games, and they believed that athletes were stupid people who couldn't do anything else. They didn't like it when they saw Sam spend time playing sports instead of studying.

They told Sam that he was making a mistake, that sports couldn't lead to anything. Soon they felt that Sam was spending too much time playing and not studying enough. Then Sam's parents insisted that he stop playing altogether.

Sam couldn't believe it. He had been getting better and better, and the other kids liked having him on their teams. He had made a whole bunch of new friends, and he loved playing with them.

On the first day of his punishment, Sam came home and went straight to his room. He wouldn't speak to his mother. He sat in his room without opening a book. When his father came home, he looked in on Sam and saw him just staring into space. He asked why Sam wasn't studying.

"I'm not going to study," Sam said, "and you can't make me."

"Why don't you want to study?" his father asked.

"If I can't play, I don't want to study, either," Sam said.

"Playing won't make you a doctor," his father said.

"Studying all the time won't make me any friends," Sam said.

Sam's father went to consult with Sam's mother. After talking for a while, they called Sam in. His father explained that he had become concerned when Sam completely neglected his studies in favor of playing. Sam agreed that he had done that. "But it's so much fun," he said.

"We want you to have fun, but you can't have all fun and no work," his father said.

Sam said he understood that.

Together, Sam and his parents decided that Sam would be allowed to play a certain number of hours per day as long as he got all his schoolwork done satisfactorily.

What would you have done if you were Sam? What would you have done if you were Sam's parents?

RACHEL'S STORY

Rachel, nine, was very happy. She had lots of friends and she did well in school. Her parents, though, thought she ought to be doing better.

"You have so much potential and you're not using it," they told her.

Rachel loved her parents and wanted their approval. But every time she did something, whether it was taking a test or preparing a science project or a book report, they told her she should have done a better job. "You're not applying yourself," she was told.

No matter what Rachel accomplished, she didn't seem to do well enough to please them. They always told her to do better next time, to improve.

It got so bad that Rachel's friends noticed the change in her. They asked her if something was wrong. Even Rachel's teachers noticed it. She had always been such a cheerful girl. Now the cheerfulness was gone.

All Rachel could think about was how bad she felt. No matter what she did, she thought, it wouldn't satisfy her parents.

One night after she knew that Rachel would be in bed, Rachel's principal stopped by to talk with her parents. The principal said that everyone had noticed a big change in Rachel, and she wanted to know if things were all right at home.

Rachel's parents were surprised to hear this. Everything was fine, they told her. But as they talked more, Rachel's parents also began to realize that their daughter had changed a little bit, and they began to understand why.

Rachel's parents felt terrible. Her father remembered that his parents had treated him the same way, and he had hated it and vowed not to do it to his own child.

When the principal left, her parents went into Rachel's room and woke her up. They talked for about an hour, and that night Rachel slept better than she had for a long time.

Do you think your parents are too easy on you, too hard on you, or just right?

ARTHUR'S STORY

Arthur, seven, often fell asleep in class. When his teacher, Mr. King, talked about subjects which Arthur already knew well, he got bored and put his head down on his hands. Soon he was asleep.

Mr. King warned Arthur about falling asleep. He made Arthur stay after class one day and told him he would be punished if he fell asleep again. Arthur told him that he couldn't help it, but Mr. King thought that Arthur just didn't care about school.

When Arthur fell asleep again after his warning, Mr. King called Arthur's parents in for a meeting. He told them that Arthur had a behavior problem. Arthur's parents were shocked. Arthur seemed so bright and alert at home, they told him. Mr. King was surprised to hear that and decided to ask Arthur in to the meeting.

He asked Arthur whether he was bored. Arthur said yes.

"When do you get bored?" Mr. King asked.

"Every time you teach something I already know," Arthur said.

"You mean, you already know what I've been trying to teach to the rest of the class? Most of your classmates still don't get it," Mr. King said.

"Well, I do," Arthur said.

Then Mr. King understood. What other kids learned only through repetition, Arthur learned the first time.

Arthur's parents told Mr. King that they had been working with Arthur for a long time, so that he would have a head start in school.

They all realized that each of them was a little bit at fault for the misunderstanding. Mr. King should have realized long before that Arthur was bored because he already knew the lessons, not that he was lazy. And Arthur's parents agreed that they should have told Mr. King about their lessons at home. Arthur himself said that he should have told Mr. King that he was bored and needed a bigger challenge.

Arthur was given more advanced work to challenge him and no longer fell asleep in class.

Have you ever been bored in class? Why?

VANESSA'S STORY

Vanessa, seven, was told that she was going to skip a grade in school. She had been doing so well in her present grade that the teacher felt school was not presenting a big enough challenge to her. Her parents were pleased with her achievements, and they wanted to make sure that Vanessa was getting everything out of school she could.

The problem was that skipping a year meant that Vanessa would be in the same grade as her older brother, Howard. He was just an average student.

When Howard's friends found out about Vanessa moving into his grade, they teased him terribly. He was embarrassed and humiliated. He told his parents that he refused to go to school. Vanessa heard about that and told them that she wouldn't go to school either if it meant embarrassing Howard.

Their parents didn't know what to do. They decided that they had made a mistake. The mistake wasn't in saying yes to Vanessa skipping a grade, but in making the decision without first consulting the whole family.

Vanessa and Howard's parents said that they were very proud of both their children. Then they explained that Vanessa wasn't being challenged by school anymore. In order for her to be challenged, she would have to skip a grade.

"Just because Vanessa may move up a year doesn't mean we love her more than Howard," their father said.

"And it doesn't make Vanessa better than Howard," said their mom.

Vanessa said that she would like to skip, but that she did not want to hurt her brother.

Howard thought about what everyone had said, then told them that he wanted Vanessa to be in the same grade. "I could show you the ropes," he said. "And I could protect you."

"What will you do if your friends say something?" his father asked.

"I'll just tell them that we're a special family," Howard said. "And I'll remind them that Vanessa's younger than they are, too."

Would it be hard for you if your brother or sister were in the same grade?

ETHAN'S STORY

Ethan was seven. His favorite programs on television were cartoons. As soon as he came home from school, he turned on the television so that he could watch cartoons. He even woke up especially early on Saturdays because that's when the best cartoons were on.

His parents, though, thought that Ethan was watching too much television and not devoting enough time to his studies. Even when he explained to them that he'd already done his homework, they still insisted that he not watch so much television. Ethan argued with his parents over how much television he should be allowed to watch.

"TV is bad for you," his father said.

"Why, what's so bad about it?" Ethan asked.

"You can find better things to do with your time," his father said. "Why don't you try reading?"

"I do read," Ethan said. "I read a lot."

"Well, read more," said his father. "From now on you'll read instead of watching television when you get home."

Ethan started to protest, but his father interrupted him. "Case closed," his father said.

Ethan went along with his father's order, but he didn't like it. He missed his favorite cartoons and he missed talking about them with his friends. But what bothered him more than anything was seeing his mother and father watching television all the time.

As soon as dinner was over, Ethan was expected to go to his room to study, but his parents sat in front of the TV all night. Finally, Ethan confronted them.

"How come it's O.K. for you to watch television all the time, but not me?" he asked.

"What do you mean?" his father said.

"As soon as you get home you turn on the TV," Ethan explained. "And you and Mom sit there all night."

Ethan's father had never thought about it before, but Ethan was right. "Well, we're adults, and you're a kid," he said.

"What's the difference?" Ethan wanted to know.

Ethan's father really couldn't think of a difference that would apply to watching television. He also couldn't remember the last book he had read. Neither could Ethan's mother.

Ethan's parents talked over the situation between themselves. His father remembered how much he had hated it when he was Ethan's age and his father told him to do something different from what he did himself. He had thought his father was a hypocrite.

Ethan's parents called Ethan into the room. "We've decided that you're right," Ethan's father said. "What's good for you is good for us. If you're going to be a good son, then we have to be good parents."

Ethan was very happy. He thought that his parents were going to tell him that he could watch TV again. Instead, they said something else entirely. "No more TV for any of us," his father said. "We'll all read from now on."

"And," said his mother, "we're going to begin tonight, right after dinner, by reading a book together. What would you like us to read, Ethan?"

What book do you think he chose? What book would you choose to read with your family?

JANE'S STORY

Jane, ten, had her heart set on being a doctor when she grew up. She used her allowance money to buy a microscope and a chemistry set. Every time she got a cut or a scrape she put some blood on a slide and looked at it under the microscope.

Her parents thought Jane should be a lawyer. They told her that it would be a waste not to use her wonderful speaking ability. They wanted her to begin taking public-speaking classes.

"But that's not what I'm interested in," Jane protested.

"But that's what you're best in," her father told her.

They fought this way for several months. Finally, her parents sought the advice of Jane's school principal. The principal told Jane's parents that Jane was too young to make a firm decision about what she wanted to be. Jane's father agreed, believing that his judgment was correct.

"But she's also too young for you to decide," the principal told him. She explained that while they're young, children should be allowed to explore whatever directions they want concerning a career. "She might change her mind fifteen or twenty times between now and college," the principal said.

When he got home, Jane's father told her that she was free to choose whatever direction she wanted, and that she would have his complete love and support.

What do you want to be when you grow up? Do you think your parents would approve?

OSCAR'S STORY

Oscar, nine, had always been interested in magic. He liked to watch magicians on television and told his friends that one day he would be a famous magician.

A couple of Oscar's friends also liked magic. As it happened, they were some of the best students in school. Often, other students would make fun of them for being "bookworms."

Oscar's father got the idea to start an after-school class for all the kids who were interested in magic. On the first day of the magic class, Oscar and his friends couldn't wait for school to end so that they could go learn about magic. When the bell rang, they went running out to catch the bus to take them to the class. "Where are you bookworms going?" another kid said.

"To take a magic class," Oscar said.

The kids all laughed, then teased Oscar and his friends until the bus came. The class was great, and the boys all enjoyed it, but the next day the other kids teased them again. When the boys ran to catch the bus, the mean kids were there again too.

A few weeks later, one of the bullies told Oscar and his friends that they weren't allowed to take the bus to magic class anymore unless they each paid him a quarter. Oscar thought about it for a second, then said O.K. His friends looked at him as if he were crazy.

Oscar took a quarter from his pocket and showed it to the bully. Then, using a trick he had learned in magic class, Oscar handed him the coin—and it disappeared.

His friends thought the bully would hit Oscar, but the boy just smiled. "That was pretty good," he said. "Where'd you learn that?"

"In magic class," Oscar said.

"Really?" the bully said.

"Yeah, it's fun. Why don't you come along with us?" Oscar said. His friends groaned. But the boy said he would.

They all got on the bus together. Oscar said he wanted to show the other kid another trick before they got to class.

"Yeah? What?" the bully said.

"I'm going to make you disappear," Oscar said, and everyone laughed.

What special subject not offered in school would you like to study?

NORA'S STORY

Nora, eight, was always very good in school. She earned high marks and got used to constant praise from her parents and teachers for doing well. She came to think of herself as someone who always does the very best. And she always did.

As she got a little older, Nora started to avoid doing anything that was new and unfamiliar. When she and several of her friends were invited to go horseback riding one Saturday, Nora refused to go.

She had never been riding before.

No one thought this was strange; they just thought she didn't feel up to it. Nora didn't tell them she was afraid that she would not be as good at it as she had always been at everything else.

A few weekends later, Nora was invited along with a group of the kids on a waterskiing trip. Again, Nora refused.

This time her mother got suspicious. She saw the look on Nora's face all weekend, and knew that Nora had really wanted to go.

"Why didn't you go with your friends?" her mother asked her.

"I just didn't feel like it," Nora said.

"Something tells me you're not telling the whole truth," her mother said. She looked straight into Nora's eyes. "Mothers know these things."

Finally, Nora admitted that people thought of her in a certain way, and she didn't want to let anybody down.

"What way is that?" her mother asked.

"They think of me as always being good, as being the best at everything. And I can't be the best at something I've never done before."

Nora's mother tried to explain to her that everyone else did not have that image of Nora; Nora had that impression of herself. "No one expects you always to be the best at everything," her mother said. "We want you to try many things. No one is good at everything, and you can't be good at something you haven't tried."

Nora agreed but said that she was scared of what people would think.

"People will think that you're a wonderful little girl who is adventurous and wants to explore, that's what they'll think," her mother said. Nora said she liked that.

Are you always willing to try new things? Are you afraid to try some things?

BORIS'S STORY

Boris, ten, wanted to be an archaeologist. He liked to dig, looking for Indian artifacts. He lived in Arizona, near the desert, where the Shoshone Indian tribe had lived for hundreds of years. When Boris found arrowheads or broken pottery, he took them home and studied them with the help of several books his parents had bought for him.

Boris thought he knew everything there was to know about the Shoshone, and proudly displayed his collection of artifacts in a bookcase in his bedroom.

On weekends, and sometimes after school, Boris would go into the desert to try to find more pieces to add to his collection. His hobby did not make him very popular with the other kids at school, who did not understand Boris's fascination with artifacts. They wondered why he didn't prefer playing with them to wandering around in the desert. They thought he was weird.

Whenever Boris brought someone his own age over to look at the things in his bookcase, he always heard the same thing: "What's the big deal? It's just a bunch of old junk."

It seemed to Boris that only adults appreciated his hobby. Mrs. Kraven, his teacher, shared his interests and encouraged him.

One day, while digging carefully, with his hands, in an area where he had once found several pieces of broken pottery, Boris uncovered what seemed to be the badly shattered bits of an urn or jar.

Boris was very excited. He reburied the shards, then drew himself a map so that he could find the site again. At home he checked his books and discovered that the urn was of a very rare type. If it could be restored, it would be worthy of museum display.

He could hardly wait to tell Mrs. Kraven what he had found, and the very next day he showed her the book and told her about his discovery. Mrs. Kraven agreed that it could be a significant find, and she offered to excavate it properly.

That afternoon Boris and Mrs. Kraven went out to the site. Mrs. Kraven knew how to remove the shards, how to make a proper record of their location and excavation, and how to protect them once they were unearthed. Boris was fascinated, watching how carefully the pieces had to be handled and how careful Mrs. Kraven was not to disturb the surrounding area.

"There may be many other things buried here," Mrs. Kraven said. "I think the museum and the university's Archaeology Department will be very interested in your urn."

The next day Mrs. Kraven said to Boris, "I took the shards to the head of the Archaeology Department. Your urn is every bit as special as you thought—a major find! He's going to start working on it right away, and told me to invite you to go over and watch, and maybe help figure out how the pieces go together."

Boris was on cloud nine all the way home. He almost didn't notice the newspaper reporters and photographers who were waiting to talk to him.

Boris was a celebrity. But what was important to him was finding the urn and helping people learn more about the Shoshone.

Have you ever done anything really special? How did you feel?